JUST BE

"A Young Man's Journey to Finding Himself"

RICHARD KEVIN BENNETT

Copyright © 2018 by Richard K. Bennett
All rights reserved. This book or any portion thereof may not be reproduced or used in any manner whatsoever without the express written permission of the publisher except for the use of brief quotations in a book review.

Limits of Liability and Disclaimer of Warranty

The author and publisher shall not be liable for your misuse of this material. This book is strictly for informational and educational purposes. The purpose of this book is to educate and entertain. The author and/or publisher do not guarantee that anyone following these techniques, suggestions, tips, ideas, or strategies will become successful. The author and/or publisher shall have neither liability nor responsibility to anyone with respect to any loss or damage caused, or alleged to be caused, directly or indirectly by the information contained in this book.
Views expressed in this publication do not necessarily reflect the views of the publisher.

Printed in the United States of America

JDB Publishing Company
ISBN: 978-0-692-19907-7

Dedication

I would like to dedicate this book to my family; I appreciate you for standing right beside me in all that I have been through. I also would like to dedicate it to my mother Charlotte Alderson, I Love You! To thousands of children whose lives I have touched over the past twenty years, but most importantly the ones who have touched my life in a very special way. Also, special thanks to my mentors and friends, you know who you are.

THANK YOU

Table of Contents

Dedication 5

Introduction 9

Chapter 1: Child's Play 12

Chapter 2: Wonder Years 27

Chapter 3: Street Life & The Dope Game 35

Chapter 4: Jessica 45

Chapter 5: My Wife Is Back 58

Chapter 6: Learning Marriage 64

Chapter 7: Church ABCs 69

Chapter 8: Growing In Faith 77

Chapter 9: Purpose 88

Chapter 10: Conclusion 94

Introduction

"Why I wrote this book. What it is and what it isn't".

The reason I decided to write this book is to share my journey to discovering who I really am. This has been a long journey, and I have not fulfilled my purpose yet, but I feel I am on the right road. Although I press daily, the road on this journey can sometimes be long and rough. This road sometimes has potholes and unforeseen curves. I will continue because to give up in the middle of this journey is unacceptable. Some people will say this is a book about my testimony, you may choose to see it that way as well. I believe it is a book that shares not only my personal truths but also how I came into establishing those truths. I will forewarn you of the language and vernacular of my younger years maybe be alarming to some, but this is my "truth". However, you will see my language change as I mature in Christ and the understanding of my True Self.

It is not a book to get you to submit to my truths, or believe what I believe. It is also not a religious book. I will not be preaching to you or trying to convert you to my personal belief. Again, I will only share my personal truths so we may find some common thread that connects us as human beings.

~"Raise a child in the way they are to go, and when he is old, he will not stray far from it". ~

Proverbs 22:6

Chapter One
CHILD'S PLAY

I was born July 28, 1966, in Chattanooga, Tennessee. My parents are Richard Raymond Bennett and Charlotte Jean (Bennett) Alderson. I have one sister from this union Deborah, who we call Debbie; she is five years older than me. I grow up on the west side of Chattanooga during segregation, so the majority of the people living around me were black. We lived in the Grove Street Apartments at 1117 Grove Street, Apartment D. College Hill Courts Housing Development was down the street, but separate from where I lived. By all accounts, I thought we had a pretty good life. I always had everything I needed and most of the things I wanted. Those around me viewed me as very fortunate. I really never knew struggle, or that there was even any dysfunction in my family, I thought it was just the way it was and I was never around anyone who lived any differently. I had a block view of the world, I didn't know a different world and different perspectives existed out there for me to explore.

My parent both had what was considered, "good jobs". My father worked for Wheeling Foundry, which at the time was considered one of the best jobs a black person could have in Chattanooga, during that time. Once I started school, my mother started working at Coke Cola Bottling Company. I really don't remember spending a lot of "family time" with my parents, they were always working. My mother made sure I was always busy with sports, I guess to keep me out of trouble.

I attended James A. Henry Elementary School and started playing football in the sixth grade. I do not remember three years of my childhood, I guess you could say those memories were suppressed. According to my mom and sister, I grew up in a household, where domestic violence was frequent. My father was what you could call "a womanizer"; he had several affairs and many outside children that my mother did not know about. He was very controlling and often fought my mother for no reason at all. My father was rarely home, he would spend days away from home, which my mother says, "Where the most peaceful time during their marriage". My father would forbid my mother to go anywhere without him and would question my sister and me about what she did, where she went and who she talked to when he was away.

One day my sister came home from school and told my mother a boy in her class said he was her brother because they had the same last name. This upset her very much, so the next day, she brought the boy and his brother home with her to meet my mother. It did not take long to conclude that he was telling the truth. Not only was he our brother, but his name was also Richard Bennett and his brother was named Ricky. Devastated, my mother called my father and the truth came out. It was undeniable; Ricky looked exactly like my dad. He had told these children he was their "uncle", but yet gave them his name. I accepted them as my older brothers, something I had always wanted, but my mother and sister did not feel the same. As time went on more children came out of nowhere, more Richards appeared until we lost count. This sealed the fate of my parent's marriage.

See my mother married my dad when she was only sixteen years old and he was more than ten years older than her. She was beautiful, but still a child. My mother says from day one, the marriage was built on control and manipulation. She believed he was her Knight in shining armor, but turned out to be her biggest nightmare. She had eleven brothers and sisters and felt she always had to fight for everything she got. Her parents worked all the time and her dad would sometimes take the money and spend it on alcohol, so there was always a lack; lack of food, clothing, and attention. When she met my dad, he showered her with "things". She thought she had hit the jackpot. Her parents signed for her to get married, unaware they were giving their daughter to a person who had not totally revealed who he was. He controlled where she went, who she could be around and how long she could stay, basically isolating her from her friends and family. Ten minutes after saying "I do", he gave her a laundry list of "can't do's". She was miserable for a long time. She only knew of one daughter, my sister Mary, who was not much younger than my mom. Needless to say, I have several older sisters and brothers, at least four are the same age as my sister Debbie, so it turns out, I went from the baby of my family to more like the middle child. I have sisters and brothers more than fifteen years younger than me.

The fussing and fighting became more frequent, probably because my dad was covering up all the things he was doing and all the children my mom didn't know about. Now as I look back, I know it was definitely because he didn't know who he truly was. During that time, being unfaithful was just what "some" men believed being a man was all about; "the hunt and pursuit", getting as many notches on your belt as possible; which was just what my dad taught me. The problem was thirteen children were left behind with no man to acknowledge them, affirm them, teach them, protect them and truly love them.

Whenever our parents would start fussing, my sister would grab my hand and we would go to our room until everything was over. Although I was sheltered from these fights by my sister, the abuse of my mother continued, until one day in 1975, when she had enough. There is a saying, "Enough is enough and too much stinks." My parent's marriage was definitely stinking. My father started fussing about something, my sister grabbed my hand and we ran off to hide in the room. I don't remember hearing a shot or getting hit by a bullet, but according to my mom, she was sick and tired, she had gotten a gun from somewhere, and when my dad slapped her, she pulled it out and fired several times at my dad, he wrestled the gun out of her hand and ran out the house. I use to hear people say, "Bullets don't have eyes", well one of those bullets had its eyes set on me. I never saw it coming and I never felt it enter my body and neither did my mom have any idea that the 32 caliber bullet had entered my body.

Unaware of what had happened; my mom, my sister and I left our house that night to go stay with her sister. My mother had made up her mind to leave my dad for good, which was probably for the best. That night I went to bed as normal, with no signs that I was wounded; no pain or blood. My mother said, in the middle of the night, something woke her up and told her to go check on me, I now know that something was the "Holy Spirit". She said I was sweating so badly that my pajamas were soaked. She got me up and rushed me to the emergency room. I had started to experience severe stomach pains; I thought it was the Krystal's I had eaten before going to bed. Once at the emergency room, the doctors did what they thought was a thorough exam, but couldn't find any reason for the severe stomach pains. My mom said one of the doctors even teased, "I think we have a big baby on our hand mom, but to make sure, we will do an x-ray of his tummy." They placed me on a stretcher and rolled me down a long hallway and into a room with large machines. They took several pictures of my stomach and wheeled me back to the room where my mom was waiting for me. In what seemed like a lifetime, the doctor returned with the x-ray in his hand. He snapped the film to a whiteboard and turned on a light, and there it was; the bullet, my bullet. The doctor immediately said, "Mom what is that?" My mom looked at the x-ray and instantly knew the bullet must have ricocheted off a wall and entered my abdomen. She immediately became frantic, she began to cry as she told the doctor about the fight and the gun, and before we knew it, there were twenty police officers asking my mom a hundred questions.

I was immediately taken into surgery, and doctors attempted to remove the bullet. Once inside, they discovered I had developed Pneumonia and they had to immediately close up my wound and were unable to remove the bullet. That same bullet rests inside my body to this day, as a reminder of a marriage gone wrong, the pain and frustration of an abused wife, but most of all the Grace and Mercy of a God that knew me in my mother's womb; from the foundations of this world, He had already chosen me. The enemy tried to take me out, by using my mother's anger and frustration with my dad. Had he succeeded, there would have been one life taken, and several affected; my mother and father in particular.

Unaware of everything going on, I remained in ICU at Children's Hospital for a couple of months. There were stories written in the newspaper about my shooting, mostly blaming my mother. My mom remained by my side throughout my hospital stay, she took off work to be with me every day, only going home to pack more clothes and check on my sister. There were no criminal charges brought against her, and I never blamed her for what happened to me. This was the turning point in all our lives; it was the beginning of my new life as a child of divorce.

After my parents divorced, my mother had to work even more to provide the lifestyle that my sister and I had become accustomed to. She would work from sun up to sun down and was rarely home. My sister was a teenager and spent a lot of her time with friends, which left me on my own to get into all kinds of mischief. I attended Northside Junior High, but school work was the last thing on my mind. My dad wasn't there, so I thought of myself as "the man of the house". I guess the proper name is "Latch Key Kid". I was basically on my own during the day, so when school was out, I came home, cooked myself something to eat; my favorite foods were "Charlie's Hot Franks and French Fries." My mom was strict about house cleaning, so I learned how to cook and clean up after myself. I had no interest in school, except to socialize. I was a popular guy because I played football and was pretty good at it. Every day when my mother got home, she would ask me if my homework was done, I would politely lie to her and say, "Yes mama." She was too tired to check it. I never brought my report cards home; if she remembered to ask about it, I would say I passed everything. Funny thing is I do not remember any teachers calling my house, although if they did, my mom was always at work. My dad never asked me anything about school, homework or grades, he would, however, ask, "Boy, how many girlfriends you got?" This is how a child falls through the cracks. Hard-working parents trying to make ends meet are left with no choice but to leave the child home alone.

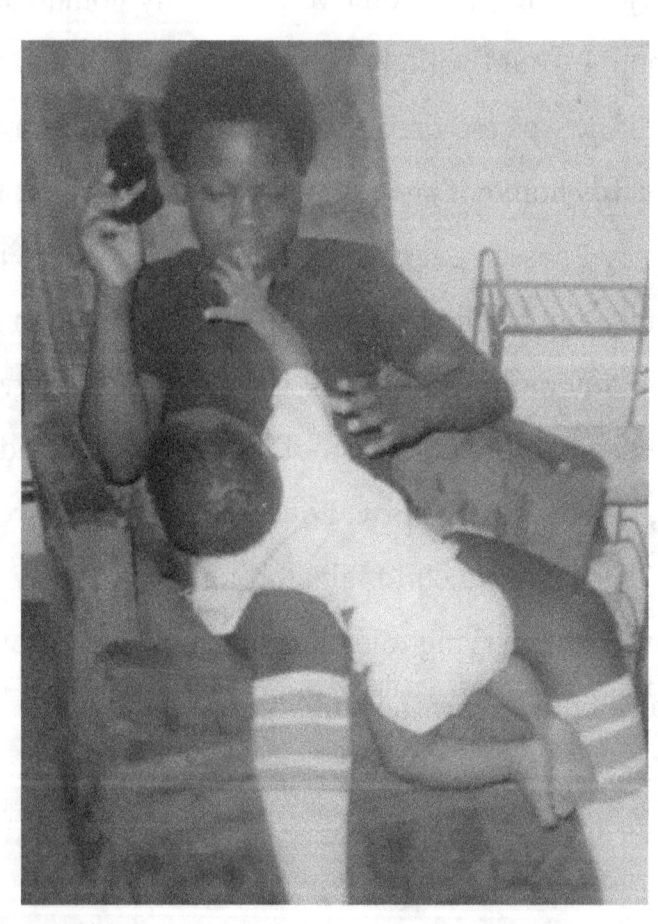

What I know now:

I did not know who I was. I didn't know I was created for greatness, therefore I settled for less than my best.
When you don't know who you are, you just exist.
I suppressed the traumatic memories from my past, without any knowledge of it.
Those memories resurfaced later in my adult life and lead to very destructive behaviors.
I had to deal with my past, in order to move forward and pave the way for my future.
You have to forgive others for the things they didn't know, and you must forgive yourself first.
I learned that no matter what I went through, both good and bad, helped to define who I am today. No experience is wasted.
Looking at the four things I learned about my childhood, it is my opinion, that these words may help you. We must teach a child "who they really are". In the Bible, it says, "We are to raise a child in the way

they are to go, and when he is old, he will not stray far from it". (Proverbs 22:6)

I have learned that parents don't always know the way to go. You can only give what you have. As a parent, if you don't know who you really are, how can you instill this in your child? It is every person's duty to discover his or her purpose for being on this planet and what you are here to do. I have forgiven my parents for the things they didn't know. I don't remember getting hugs and kisses, or even being told, "I love you". It just wasn't what my parents did. I was expected to know I was loved. A child needs to hear the words, feel the hugs and kisses, it is very important. I have talked with my mother about this, and I learned she didn't receive those things as a child herself; therefore, it was normal for her not to show affection. Now that I have my own children, it is important to my wife and me that our children know, without a doubt that they are loved. I make sure that my children are affirmed daily. As a matter of fact, they have their own affirmations that they speak over themselves daily.

AFFIRMATIONS

I am smart; I can learn anything

I am strong; I have self-control

I am safe and secure

I am loved by God, my parents,
and family

I am beautiful inside and out

I was created for greatness

I have a purpose and a destiny

I am healthy in my mind, body, and spirit

I am wealthy physically, mentally
,spiritually and financially

The gracious favor of God is on my life.

~"The heart is deceitful above all things and desperately wicked: who can know it?"~

Jeremiah 17:9

Chapter Two
"THE WONDER YEARS"

In the ninth grade, I attended City High School and continued playing football. My game got better each year. 1980-1984 my school was district champions, and I like to think my tackling skills helped to get us there. Men from my neighborhood would congratulate me on how well I played, but my father rarely came to any of my games. My mother gave me all the support she could, but her work schedule did not leave a lot of free time. Although I appreciated my mom being at my games, it wasn't the same as having the support of my father. I believe with that support and guidance, I could have made it to the NFL.

My popularity grew, while my grades continued to plummet. When I was called upon to read in class, I would cause a disturbance to get sent to the office, I did not want anyone to know I could not read. On the outside, I pretended to be a confident person, but on the inside, I was afraid of my inability to read would be exposed. I fought a lot in school, I know now it was because I did not know who I was. I fought to cover up my inadequacies and lack of self-esteem and self-worth.

Although I loved playing football, it was not all I was interested in; of course, there were also girls. God blessed me with "pretty brown eyes" and I used them to my advantage. It didn't help that I was one of the only ninth graders in my school with a car, which only helped to build my reputation as a "ladies' man". My parents bought the car so I could get back and forward from school, football practice and games, but little did they know, it was my chick magnet and it was used for more than just transportation. I was also smoking weed, selling joints in school   I had lots of girlfriends, and even at an early age, I could have a conversation with anyone. I would listen to my sister Debbie and her friends talk about boys and my mom and her sisters talk about what they wanted from a man. I took notes and used it on my girlfriends. I couldn't read, but I knew how to talk to females. I was definitely blessed with "the gift of gab".

At the beginning of my twelfth- grade year, one of my girlfriends told me she was pregnant. I wasn't upset about the pregnancy; I was actually excited. I wanted a child, I thought it would be great to be a father; all I had to do was the opposite of what I had seen. Unfortunately, neither my girlfriend nor her mother felt the same. She wanted to have an abortion. I asked my mom if she would help me, and she agreed, I begged her to let my mom and me raise the child, but she refused the offer, and she went ahead with her plans to have the abortion. I had a job after school, so I paid the money, and it was over before it had a chance.

After she had the abortion, I did not want to see her anymore, I felt like a part of me had been taken away. I didn't ever want to feel that kind of pain again. That experience made my heart hardened toward all women; I didn't care about "love", only sex.

Being a young man faced with a situation of having a child and not able to have any say in whether the child was born or not was very challenging. I thought to have a child, would give me someone on this earth who would love me no matter what. In my opinion, because I wasn't afforded the opportunity to make that decision, it caused me to say, "To Hell with Life." During this time, I had a lot to think about, the whole situation of losing a child I never knew and then there was my grades and graduation.

Although my grades sucked, and I could not read, I was passed from grade to grade because I played football so well. I would talk to my teachers into letting me tell a story in my own words, instead of reading it out loud. I would beg them to not fail me so I could continue to play football and it worked, right up to the twelfth-grade year. The only thing that stood between me and my diploma was my homeroom teacher Mrs. Shannon, if she gave me anything other than a "C", I would not graduate. I went into her classroom, I looked her in the eyes, with tears in my pretty brown eyes and said, "Please Mrs. Shannon, please I just need a "C", I have to graduate". I would have done anything to get that "C", so I was definitely not above begging and pleading with her to pass me. I didn't deserve to pass and I knew it, I hadn't even put forth an effort, but I felt not graduating would ruin my reputation, I had to graduate and I did.

I was entering the "real world", still unable to read, with a diploma in hand and my gift of gab, how far would it get me. Would I be able to continue to fake it? How would I fill out applications? Not to mention, I was asked to come to the University of Tennessee at Knoxville in the summer for football camp. I was going to college? I had never even thought about that, I was too busy trying to lie my way through high school.

    I went to a football camp, but an accident cut that short. I tore a bone in my ankle and could not play football anymore. Sadly to say, I was only a little disappointed because I knew I would not make it in college. Back in Chattanooga, what would I do? I held three jobs at the same time; I would talk my way through the application process. I knew I needed more, I wasn't sure what to do to get it, but I knew college was not in the picture. I was introduced to cocaine and a new door was opened.

What I know now:

Trouble in High School

What I learned is when a child has the ability and potential to really do some great things academically and in sports, but not the self-awareness, it is easy to be lead down the wrong path.

IDENTITY IS NECESSARY!

I learned you can only hide a deficiency for so long before you eventually have to deal with it.

I am so glad I had to deal with my inability to read, now I read everything I can get my hands on.

"A person, who knows how to read but chooses not to, is no better than a person who does not know how to read".

~Mark Twain~

~ *"It is easier to build a strong child than to repair a broken man."*~

Frederick Douglass

Chapter Three
"STREET LIFE & THE DOPE GAME"

In 1984 – 1985 Crack cocaine hit the streets of Chattanooga, it was devastating to the community and eventually to me. Before I knew it, I was selling crack cocaine. I did not know being introduced to cocaine would be the doorway to destruction. I remember starting out with powder cocaine, I was still selling weed at that time, nickel bags, dime bags, twenty-cent pieces, half ounces, whatever they wanted. Because of my popularity, and my reputation, I had favor with people on the street. Today, the older guys I ran with would be considered OGs, guys like Tony, Kenny, Edward, and others. They knew me from the streets and from playing football, so after graduating high school, it was nothing for me to get into that life. I would be in the clubs, hanging out, just doing what I did.

A typical day for me was hanging out, drinking, smoking weed, snorting cocaine, making money, buying new clothes, and WOMEN. This went on every day, and

then days turned to weeks, and weeks into months, and months into years. I was dealing with several women, which brought about many crazy circumstances and situations. With this lifestyle came, drama and often violence, many times it couldn't be avoided, because, in order to stay in the game, you couldn't let anybody get away with anything; especially disrespect. To maintain a reputation, identity, or street credit in their hood, a person would not only fight, but also shoot, and stab you; to hold on to that rep, they would even kill you, and for some reason, women loved that, and men respected that.
One day this dude came and got three-sixteenths from me, which was the equivalent of three hundred dollar worth of dope. I repeatedly told him, "look, man, you better bring my money back, and I don't want to hear any excuses." On the day, he was supposed to pay me, he didn't, he said "I had to pay some bills and don't have your money", so I hit him in the mouth, knocked him down, went in his pocket, he had just got paid, he had about five hundred and thirty something dollars. I got my three hundred dollars, threw the rest on his chest, told him, "N----, I don't f--- with you no mo."

Violence was a norm, I remember one time I was in a shootout. I was hanging out with my partners, and we had been drinking and snorting cocaine all night, and we were extremely high; there were some dudes that kept trying to get at us. One thing led to another, and we started shooting back and forth. Because I was so high, I had no fear, just foolishness, so I step out from behind the car and started busting, that means I just starting shooting, I got hit and had to be taken to the hospital. Thank God it wasn't too bad just a graze, the doctors sewed me up and kicked me out.

Living a life where there was always drugs, and lots of money, there would always be women. As a drug dealer, there was never any lack of women who were willing to do whatever they had to in order to get dope, money or the man. My partners and I would have our own private strip shows. I was amazed at the people I met while selling drugs; there were doctors, lawyers, teachers, mothers, fathers; strung out on dope, and willing to do whatever it took to get it.

This street life was good at the time, I had money, women and plenty of partners who I thought had my back, it lasted until I got caught, or should I say I actually did not get caught, I was set up. 280 crack rocks were found in the car of the dude I was riding with, on my way to see a woman. They charged me with possession of crack cocaine for resale, and I had to serve some time. When I was released, I was put on 10 years probation. I had to pay a substantial amount of restitution to get my life back. During those 10 years, a lot happened, and I started to recognize something about myself. There were some things I wanted to change because I knew this dope game wasn't going to last.

After getting caught with drugs, I couldn't seem to get back on my feet in the dope game. At one time, I had $84,000 cash money and a kilo of fresh powder cocaine. I thought I was on top of things because I had nice cars, plenty of money, and plenty of women. The more I tried to regain my status in the drug game, the more I failed. The more I failed, the more cocaine I snorted, and the more weed I smoked.

During this time in my life, so many things happened to me, there are some things I would love to tell you, but I can't because "a person's perceptions are their reality", and people always try to connect you to your past. There will be some people who will read this book and know exactly what I am talking about. During the seven years, I was caught up, not many people really knew. I was able to maintain, or so I told myself. In the beginning, it wasn't bad; I would still snort cocaine, smoke a little weed, but not many people knew what was going on. The truth is I was what you call "Undercover". I went to work and did what I had to do, but I knew inside this wasn't me.

It got really hard to keep up the appearance, it was hard to "maintain". It took my mom turning her back on me, to make me realize I had hit rock bottom. I had been shot several times, sold drugs, on drugs, but now I was really tired of being sick and tired. I can remember my mother's word, when 12 carloads of police pulled up and bomb-rushed her house, accusing me of robbing a Subway. My mother's words to me were; "You will never amount to shit and never be shit, GET OUT OF MY HOUSE!"

After hanging in the streets, selling dope, gaining the respect of the streets, I was feeling like I was on top of the world. It took my mom turning her back on me to make me realize in gaining the respect of the streets, I had lost the respect of my mother and my family. I was no more than a common criminal, street thug, and drug dealer. It is so amazing how you think you know something, think you are so smart, and got it all together, and then LIFE HAPPENS.

After several months of being estranged from my family and living with various women, I was determined to prove my mother wrong. I called her and asked her if I could use her address as a place of residence because I was going to apply for a job. I went to Chattanooga Tent Company, where I inquired about a job and I was hired. The owners helped me get my CDL licenses, as a matter of fact, I couldn't read well, so they really "grandfathered" me in and gave me my licenses because I had already been driving for them.

For nine years, I drove trucks all over the country, setting up tents at all types of events such as "Church Hills Downs", and the "Kentucky Derby". These were nothing like camping tents; they were beautiful ballrooms, with dance floors, chandeliers, and air conditioning. I have always been a great worker, and I enjoyed that job and felt a great sense of accomplishment, and I did my best. We even won awards for the tents, I was very proud of the work we did.

Even at this point in my life, I still was dipping and dapping with cocaine. Although I worked, I was still trying to sell dope, because I was still using it. I continued to find myself in very crazy relationships with various irrational women, which led to fights, even had one try to stab me because she thought she was the only one I loved. It was really a wild time of trying to find myself and show my mom she was a liar. I was looking at life through very foggy lenses, and trying to make things come clear.

I remember thinking, "man this is fucked up, and I need to turn this around." In my eyes, I had been winning, but not knowing who I was, low self-esteem, and bad images had caught up with me. Trying to get back to something that wasn't even real in the first place is not only hard, but it is also impossible because you are delusional and what you see is only a mirage. Looking back on this reminds me of a Bible verse; "And you shall know the truth and the truth shall set you free." (John 8:32) I had heard the word "Free" but really didn't understand what it was. I didn't get it, but now after all the hell I've been through and think I would lose everything, including my mind, I now understand. The freedom comes when you know without a shadow of a doubt, "God loves you and He has you no matter what", and every day I live, I am learning what that looks like.

What I know now:

There are many ways to make money and when you don't understand money and how it works you are in my opinion doomed to always need it.

It is important to understand the family, what it is and how it works. I wanted a family, but at this point, I was not ready. I did not have the necessary tools to run my own house. I didn't have an ear to hear God; therefore I had no instructions or vision.

"For if a man know not how to rule his own house, how shall he take care of the church of God.
 Not a novice, lest being lifted up with pride he falls into the condemnation of the devil. (1 Timothy 3:5-6) When you don't know who you are, you are subject to whatever. Eyes wide open, but cannot see anything, you have no vision and vision is given by GOD, not man.

~" Not a novice, lest being lifted up with pride he falls into the condemnation of the devil."~

1 Timothy 3:5-6

Chapter Four
"JESSICA"

I was almost thirty years old, but still not yet a man. I wanted a family, not just my mom and sister, but my own family; a wife and children, but I had to grow up, become a man, stop acting like a fool, fall out of love with the streets, and be willing to do the work it would take and have the open mindset to see things from a worldview and not just a block view.

I was still working at Chattanooga Tent Company and had worked my way up to second-shift supervisor. One night after I got off work, I decided to go and hang out with some of my homies. We had plans to start on Ninth Street, now called MLK Jr. Blvd. We would go from club to club then end up at a popular after-hours spot. We pulled up at the first club on our list, Club 25; we smoked a joint outside and then headed in. I grabbed a seat at the bar, ordered a Schlitz Malt Liquor Bull, and was kicking it until this Shorty walked in. When I turned around and saw her, a thought went through my mind; "Damn There

Go, My Wife". What? I am not sure where that thought came from, because I never wanted to be married in my life. Our eyes met and she came over to talk to me. She about 5feet 4, with a black leather skirt and vest on, she was very attractive and had a beautiful smile.

She introduced herself, "Hey my name is Jessica, what's your name?" I told her my name was Richard, and then she continued on with a laundry list of questions. She wanted to know a lot of things about me, she asked, "Are you married?", "Do you have children?" "Do you have a girlfriend?" I answered NO to each of her questions, then she smiled and said; "Are you sure?" "Am I sure, of course, I'm sure", I said, and then she continued with her questions. "Do you have a job?" "Where do you work?" "How long have you worked there?" I almost felt like I was being interrogated, but even when I got arrested the police didn't ask me this many questions, but she was cute and interesting so I played along and told her what she wanted to know. We continued to talk for about thirty or forty-five minutes, then my partners said they were ready to go. We exchanged numbers, I told her I would call her, I wasn't ready to go because I was enjoying the conversation, but I wasn't driving so I had to leave.

Ninth Street was a popular hangout spot and back in the day businesses on Ninth Street was black-owned. There clubs and restaurants on both sides of the street. You could go from spot to spot and never had to move your car. The Whole Note, The Half-Note, Memos, Club 25, Roses, and Lamar's, to name a few. After we left the club, we went down the street to another club, and a few minutes later, in walks this young lady. It was so crazy, our eyes met again and we both started laughing. She came over to me and said, "I thought you were on your way home". I replied, "I'm not driving, I have to go where they go". We started talking and picked right up where we had left off, believe it or not, she had more questions. Once again, after about one hour my friends were ready to leave, so we said our goodbyes again. Back in the car, thinking I was headed home when one of my homies made the suggestion to go to the "after-hours club". It was the hangout spot everyone went to when all the clubs closed. It stayed open until 5 or 6 in the morning. I was game for whatever; I didn't have to go to work the next day so we went. I bought a beer and set down at a table. There was music playing and people dancing. I wasn't a stranger to this place, so there were other people there I knew. I started talking to some young ladies and turned around and she was standing there. "Now I know you are following me", I said to her, she smiled and said, "No, my friend wanted to come in here, this isn't my kind of place". She went to the bar, and as she was standing there, a guy I knew put his arms around her waist. I said, "Hey Bruh, she's with me!" She turned and looked at me and she said, "Oh I'm with you, excuse me, I didn't know that." We both laughed and continued to talk the rest of the night until it was time for her to leave. She was sweet but feisty. I could tell she could hold her own. Believe it or not, she had to be at work at 5am. She left at 4:30 heading to work. I hung out a couple more hours with my homies, before going home.

When I woke up later that morning, I gave her a call to make sure she gave me the right number. She answered the phone, she told me she was very tired and was still at work. I invited her over to watch some movies. She told me her clutch was acting up in her car, but really she had bought a car she didn't know how to drive, so she burnt the clutch. I offered to call her a taxi to my house because my car was down also. She ended up having to work twelve hours and was exhausted. Once she got off work, she went home, took a shower and rode a taxi to my house. When the taxi pulled up, she got out, I paid the driver and we walked into the house. I offered her some food and something to drink because I knew she had been working all day and was tired. I pulled out several movies and ask her which movie she wanted to watch. I really wasn't interested in the movies, I was really ready to get back to the conversation because, at that time in my life, I really didn't talk a lot, but I felt really comfortable talking to her.

She was very tired after being awake for over 24 hours. So twenty minutes into the movie, she fell asleep and she slept for eight hours. After the movie went off, I decided to holler at one of my partners down the street, so I went and hung out with him for twenty-thirty minutes, smoked a joint and drunk some beer. After we were done, I walked back to the house and this perfect stranger that I felt I had known all my life was still laying on my bed peacefully asleep. I watched two more movies before she woke up. When she finally woke up she was so ashamed that she had fallen asleep and had stayed all night. I told her it was all good, she said, "I have never done anything like this before". I reassured her that I knew she was telling me the truth and I didn't think badly of her. Within a 24-hour period, I was having a feeling of "deep like" for her. She knew nothing about me being a drug dealer and drug user. She had no idea I had shot people and had been shot four times. She didn't know all the things I had been through and had taken other people through. I couldn't help but wonder how she would feel about me if she did. I decided not to tell her, I thought I would ride it out as long as I could.

After our night together, she told me I should not feel obligated to call or see her again. When she left, she said she was taking the taxi to see her friend, so I called her a taxi, gave her the fare and told her to call me when she got there. I found out later from her friend, that her coming to see me in a taxi was not something she would ever do. So that gave me the perception that she was feeling me like I was feeling her. For months, we were inseparable. The more we were together; more of my life was being revealed.

One day we bumped into a mutual friend, and Jessica was so excited, he was a person she had been waiting for me to meet because she didn't know I already knew him. As soon as we pulled up, Jessica excitedly introduced us, "Rob this is Richard, Richard this is Rob." I got out the car approached him and said, "I know this n---- his name is Stump". Jessica was shocked, she said, " I wanted y'all to meet, Rob and I are really good friends". Jessica later told me, Rob was gesturing to her the "crazy" sign behind my back. He called her later and asked her where in the hell she had met me. He told her to stay away from me because I was a violent person. Fortunately, she didn't believe him; she had seen my heart and had fallen in love with the real me.

The more we were seen with each other, the more questions she had about my life before her. We would never say we were in a relationship, or that we were boyfriend and girlfriend; we decided to call it a "Comfortable Situation". I was comfortable with her and she was comfortable with me. It was just implied that we were in a monogamous relationship. In fact, we were always together. When we weren't at work, we were either at her house or she was at mine. We talked about everything, she told me about her past relationships and she asked me all types of questions, damn she asked me a lot of questions! She told me she had been married before, but her husband had been killed. She also talked about a dude who wouldn't leave her alone. He was on that stalking tip. I asked her where he lived, and we just happened to ride by there. I got out, knocked on his door. His mother answered the door, I asked for him and when he came outside, I let him know, he better not ever touch her or talk to her. I told him, "If you see her walking down the street, you better cross the damn street or I will hurt you!" Even to this day, she hasn't had any more problems out of him or any other man.

Moving forward in life with a woman I barely knew, but in a matter of months, I had fallen in love with. Love was a strange word to me at that time, being that I had never been in love before. Jessica was doing some soul searching in her life. She had a question about her career and where she wanted to live. She told me she never wanted to live in Chattanooga, so after a few days of thinking, she came to my job and announced to me that she had decided to go to Savannah, Georgia. I couldn't go because I was comfortable with my life, my job, and my on-the-side drug selling. I couldn't believe she was leaving, we couldn't say we were breaking up or anything because we had only been in a "comfortable situation", we kissed and I simply said to her, "My wife leaving me." That was the first time I had ever spoken something like that out loud, then she left.

After arriving in Savannah, she told me she would begin her job search the next day. We talked as often as we could the first week she was there. That weekend my partners started calling me, asking me to get out and to tell me some young ladies had been inquiring about where I had been. I was still in a daze from meeting the perfect stranger, so I told them I would holler at them the next time I was off. The next week I began to get back into the drug scene and making more sells. The time I had been spending with Jessica, I started spending that time in the streets. When the weekend rolled around again, I was ready to be my old self, hanging out with the fellows and chasing women.

It had been two weeks since Jessica had been gone. I was getting back comfortable with my life before her. I talked with her mother a couple of times; I had no idea that she might come back. Three weeks had passed and the weekend had rolled around again and I was ready to hang out and just be me. I was at work that Friday, around 8:30 that night, I returned from my break, one of the young men that work for me, gave me a message that Jessica had called and said she loved me and was on her way back home. At this point, I didn't know how to feel. I had gotten comfortable doing me and here it is the young lady I had only known a few months and had fallen in love with was on her way back home. I had some decisions to make. I said to myself, "Damn, I don't owe her nothing, she decided she needed to find herself and packed up and left, why am I feeling crazy, I should be kicking it, I am not doing anything wrong. I didn't ask her to leave and now she is coming back, what does she expect me to do?"

3 Things You Should Know Before Entering Into A Relationship:

1. Know Who You Are!
2. Have A Vision!
3. Make sure that person is a part of God's vision for your life!

"If any of you lack wisdom, let him ask God who gives generously to all without reproach and it will be given him."
~James 1:5~

Chapter Five
"MY WIFE IS BACK"

I Got the phone call that Jessica was on her way back, she had been gone for about three weeks. I never had feelings of loving nobody before; now here I was experiencing love, something I knew nothing about but I knew it was something different about this young lady. It was something about Jessica that made me want to live beyond what I have seen; beyond what I thought life could be. I felt mixed emotions, I knew she brought something special to the table but I didn't know if I should take the chance. At this point in my life, I needed to be evaluating my life values and what those were. Looking at the moment, I didn't have values or a vision, shit I just wanted to hang out and sell dope on the side and hope she would be a part of that. Here she comes, so I canceled my plans and I waited on her to get back. Once she got back to Chattanooga, she called me and came to see me. We began that same day planning our lives together. We never said we were in a relationship or that we "went together", we were too old for all that, we were back in our "Comfortable Situation". At the time, I wasn't really sure what that meant, but after spending countless hours together; learning about each other, eventually we moved in together and we were good.

Jessica asked me to go to church with her, I really wasn't feeling it. My experience with church folks wasn't good, I felt like church was something they did to ease their conscious and most of them were very phony, it really didn't mean that much to me. Sunday, was just another day of the week to me, but I did it for her. After a few months of living together, Jessica came to me and said, "I can't live like this anymore!" I was like, "Live like what?" "Everything is good baby, what are you talking about?" She said, "We are living in sin." I didn't know anything about that. I thought to myself, "Living in sin, what the hell is she talking about, we are good". She was confusing me because this was the first time I was not running here and there with different women, so I needed her to explain why she couldn't live here with me in the life we started together. I said, "Baby you are not seeing anyone else and I'm not seeing anyone else, so how are we living in sin?" Of course, she explained; she started running down her "ABC of Church Stuff". She said, she was going to church now, she was making some changes and she wanted to live right. I listened to what she said and because I was ignorant of this new lifestyle she was talking about, I said, "Ok let's do it!"

The only example of marriage I had was my parent's marriage. It wasn't really a great example. As a man, my father was the best father "he knew how to be". During my parent's marriage and totally without my mother's knowledge; my father had several outside children. I figured being married to Jessica couldn't be any more complicated than being in this "Comfortable Situation", so I agreed with living this new lifestyle. What does the bible say about a man having a wife? Oh yeah, "He who so finds a wife finds a good thing and obtains the favor of the Lord." (Proverbs 18:22) I knew I could definitely use some of that in my life, so July 26, 1996, after knowing her for only seven months, I married my soul mate. It was the best decision I have ever made. My mother and her husband, Jessica's parents, and Pastor Tommy Davis stood under a tree at the courthouse as we promised to honor, cherish and respect each other, in sickness and in health, through good time and bad. Hindsight being 20/20, I still say I didn't know what I was getting myself into. I thought this new lifestyle would be easier but I had a lot to learn.

3 Things to Understand About Marriage

1. Understand that marriage does not come with a blueprint and you can't look at someone else's to make your marriage work.

2. You have to view the beauty of individuality and see how important it is that you are different.

3. Allow your differences to bring you into the awesomeness of being one.

~"He who so finds a wife finds a good thing and obtains the favor of the Lord."~

Proverbs 18:22

Chapter Six
"LEARNING MARRIAGE"

The first year or two were challenging, actually very challenging. See we were establishing some ground rules for our new life. We were still feeling each other out. I was seeing what I could get away with and what I could not and she was kind of doing the same thing. I know as you read this, you think I wasn't doing right, but I must place a "Lol" right here, because she wasn't having it and neither was I. Yes I knew she was the one, she is bone of my bone and flesh of my flesh, and if this was true this is the foundation I would have to build on. In my heart I was already done with all that foolishness and Jessica wasn't going and for those of you who are "ebonically" challenged, "She wasn't one for playing games".

I was learning a lot about the "Church" stuff and scriptures. Matthew 19:4-6 says. "Have ye not read, that he which made them at the beginning made them male and female and said, for this cause shall a man leave his father and mother, and shall cleave to his wife; and they twain shall be one flesh. Wherefore they are no more twain, but one flesh. What therefore God hath joined together, let no man put asunder." This said to me, we couldn't use our parent's marriages as our example, but we had to learn what marriage meant to God. He expected us to become one, which was very scary to me. I wasn't sure how we were supposed to do that.

According to Jessica's "ABC's of Church Stuff"; hanging out wasn't allowed. That was extremely crazy to me because that is what I had done most of my life. Once I met her, we were together all the time, we enjoyed spending time together, so going out to clubs became less exciting or important to me. On Fridays, we would go to the store, pick up some snacks and movies and we would "Shut In", that meant "See You Monday". We didn't need any company; we had fun all by ourselves.
After not hanging out with my friends for a few months, they were like, "Damn Meat, where have you been?" "You don't even hang out with your boys anymore,

you've changed." I said, "Naw man, it ain't like that, I just been in." Seven months before, I would hang out with my dudes; we would stay out all night or for a few nights if I wanted to. But she said that was sinning and not a part of the new lifestyle. I didn't remember "hanging out" being a part of the "Do Not" list, we had NEVER discussed it; I knew I would have remembered that conversation. She was for real about this new lifestyle, she had even threatened to leave me a couple of times, and I truly didn't know what I had gotten myself into.

What I know now:

Marriage is something that cannot be taught. You both learn as you go for the rest of your life.

You must commit to a process of life with the individual you choose to marry.

In marriage, things happen that may change the direction of the marriage or that might call for a reevaluation of your plans.
- Children
- Illness
- Financial Challenges
- Unforeseen Situations

~" You hypocrite, first take the beam out of your own eye, and then you will see clearly to remove the speck from your brother's eye."~

Matthew 7:5

Chapter Seven
"CHURCH ABCs"

I Started attending service with her; at first, I wasn't really interested in what they called "Church". My concept of church wasn't what I was seeing. People were still doing what they wanted to when they wanted to but were hypocritical of everyone else's actions. They would turn up their noses and judge everyone else, but they were doing the same thing. It all felt fake and phony to me, I just didn't want to get caught up in it. We struggled for the first year or so because she had a perception of what she thought a "Godly Man" was and how he looked and acted.

As we were working through the issues in our new lifestyle, as a supervisor at my job, I had to travel a lot. I would be on the road a few weeks each month and she hated that. We were no longer having our "Shut-Ins" because I had to work. Jessica didn't have a job at the time; she says it was her way of "testing" me to see if I would be a good provider... I really didn't know what I was getting myself into. Jessica was in nursing school and was about to graduate. She was studying all the time and even when I was at home, we couldn't go anywhere because she had to study. It was a difficult year, adjusting to each other and to our new lifestyle.

The time apart was taking a toll on us and neither of us liked what was happening. Jessica came to me and asked me to quit my job. It wasn't just the fact that I was on the road a lot, she also knew I was around a lot of things and people who were not good for me and my new lifestyle. She told me I was better than that job, I could have and do so much more. I told her, "Baby if I do that, you will have to "hold me down" and take on the responsibilities until I get another job". She was willing to do that, so the next week; I turned in my keys and told them I was going to do something different. The next morning, I was up looking for another job driving trucks locally and in less than a week, I got hired on at Kitts Miller Asphalt & Paving Company. I was home in the evenings and the pay was better. I felt great about the new position. I drove asphalt trucks for them and it was exciting to be doing something different, learning new things and meeting new people. I kept the job a Kitts Miller for two years until I got a better job at Riverbend Materials.

I drove a boom truck for Riverbend Materials, delivering sheetrock all around the Southeast. During this time, Jessica and I were planning our lives together. We had several miscarriages but we continued to believe God for children. We were doing the "Church" thing regularly and I got more emerged. One Sunday, I was sitting in the pew listening to the pastor. I know it had to be the Spirit of God that pulled me right to the front of the congregation. The pastor was talking and the next thing I knew I was standing next to him. He asked me, "Why did you come today?" I said, "I really don't know, I'm just sick and tired of being sick and tired." He said, "Well we are glad to have you, man." I didn't understand why, but I began to cry. I cried for what seemed like hours and at that point, I knew something had changed in me.

I was interested in learning more, so after a couple of months went by, I went to have a conversation with the pastor. I wasn't versed in the "Church Talk", so I just said what I felt. I said, "Hey pastor, I need to talk to you and if you tell anyone what I tell you, we are going to have a problem. Look, I'm not that good at reading the bible; I need the bible on tape." He looked at me with a serious face and said, "Definitely, I will get one for you." I wasn't trying to scare him, but this had been a secret I carried for a long time. Now my secret was out, I finally told someone I couldn't read that well. I had maneuvered life by talking myself through things but this was different.

The pastor bought me the bible on tape and I began listening. I was still hanging out sometimes with my friends from the Westside of town. I would still drink a beer or smoke weed every now and then, but now instead of riding and listening to the radio, I would be listening to the bible. "In the beginning, God created the heavens and the earth and the earth was without form, and void; and darkness was upon the face of the deep", the CD continued to play. My homies thought I was crazy, they would say, "Meat, you have lost your mind man, why are you listening to the bible?" I told them, "Man if this is the truth that will sustain and change people lives and give them a life greater than they ever had before, I have to know. If this God is real, he's going to have to come and get me where I am." And where I was; was right in the hood life, it was what I knew. Grinding to have something better, If God wanted me, He was coming to the hood to change me, change my mindset and understanding of who He was. He was going to have to be my teacher. I was trying to find out who I was, and it was new to me, but I was going to go hard at it. My mindset was, "If this God or the Holy Spirit was going to change my life, I didn't have to change myself, He would. If it happens to me, then it happens."

What I Know Now

1. Life throws a lot of curves and situations. Life is neither bad nor good; it is all about your perception. You must make sure you stay focused on the things worth focusing on and not getting ahead of yourself.

2. I have found when dealing with perception, patience, and thoughts as it applies to other people's lives, it is best to deal with the beam in your own eye before dealing with the speck in your brother's eye (Matthew 7:5).

I think this is very relevant when moving forward and having a fresh perspective on life and balance. Without it we find ourselves being hypocritical and having a false narrative on life.

3. I have observed all types of different religions, Christianity, Islam, Buddhism, Hinduism, and various other looks of God.

What I know for sure is; it is very important that you find your foundation and belief in a higher power, whatever that is for you and take a firm hold, because if and when life brings about hardships, dependences, crisis, and pain, you will need that foundation to be strong and sure.

For me, my foundation rests in Yeshua Hamashiach, Jesus the Christ. My faith in God has been tested over and over, but I know that I know My God is God, and you must know the same.

~"Study to show yourself approved unto God, a workman that needed not to be ashamed, rightly dividing the word of truth."~

2 Timothy 2:15

Chapter Eight
"GROWING IN FAITH"

The more I listened, the more I learned and I knew changes were happening in me. I met a brother at the congregation and he was a very big part of my growth in the early years because he was willing to listen to me. He wasn't intimidated by the things I had done in my past; he would encourage me through whatever I was going through. He didn't judge me, he just listened. I love that brother to this day.

Years later, a man I met in a men's prayer group paid my way to seminary. I was initially excited, but once I started, I couldn't identify with the teachings. At the time I wondered why I could not grasp on wholeheartedly to the theology being taught, but as I grew in the knowledge of God and of who I am to God. I started to recognize that every image of God and Jesus I saw was white and everything associated with blackness was bad; the devil, sin, oppression or slavery. Images are very powerful, if the image I associate my higher power to is nothing like me, it is easier to succumb to the belief that as a people we are inferior or less than. I couldn't accept that, I didn't believe that this God would send His only begotten son to earth to die for people He had no stake in, people who were inferior to every other race of people. The more I studied, I learned God created one race; The Human Race. It was a man that decided we needed to be divided and labeled in order to make one race feel superior over another.

    The more I learned, the more I wanted to learn. I started studying the history of the Bible, then American history, African-American history, and world religions. I wanted to know where black people were in the bible. What part did we take as a people during that time frame? I wanted to know if there were black disciples, prophets, leaders, kings, and queens or were we simply just slaves, as we had been taught for so many years.

    The more I studied, I saw how denominations were started and in each denomination, there were rituals added or taken away to separate them from the other denominations. I found myself wanting to study every day and my reading was getting better. It was nothing but God, He taught me daily. I used to tell people, "I didn't get hooked on phonics, but I got hooked on Jesus." Not only was my mindset changing, but also my language and desires. They things I said before; were no longer a part of my vocabulary. When I saw my friends and they said, "Man you have changed" I no longer tried to prove to them that I was the same old Meat because inside I knew I was not. I had changed and it was for the better.

    No matter what I read in the Bible, the Spirit of God would translate it into the simplest form so I could understand it. I came across the scripture in 2 Timothy 2:15 "Study to show yourself approved unto God, a workman that needed not to be ashamed, rightly dividing the word of truth." That spoke to my Spirit, I knew I would learn so much more if I studied and asked God for the true interpretation.

    TRUTH is a huge word, it is imperative that we know the truth. Romans 1:25 says, "Because they exchanged the truth of God for a lie and worshipped and served the creature rather than the Creator, who blessed forever! Amen." If we don't know the Truth, we fall for anything. For example, one absolute truth for me is; to produce a child, it takes a male and a female. So the homosexual conversation never became a conflicting issue to me because this was one of the first truths I examined and received as to be absolute.

But how do we know the Truth? When we seek God, His Spirit will lead us into all Truth. I didn't depend on the pastor or anyone else; I know there was something more God would teach me; if I sought after Him. When it comes to Absolute Truth, it can only be applied to me, it is an individual thing. The truth for my life may not be a truth in someone else's life. I know now that slave owners used the bible to make slaves believe slavery was the will of God and because they were not allowed to read, they believed it.

Reading became so important to me and still is. I had been a slave, having to depend on the interpretation of others because I didn't know how to read for myself. I was at the mercy of others just like a slave; even as I write this it brings tears to my eyes. For so many years I had to rely on others to read for me. I had to trust that they were being truthful and giving me the right information. I have to Selah (pause) right here, and take a "Praise Break". I have to Thank My God for releasing me from captivity. What others took for granted, I desired for most of my life, and it means so much to me. I walked around pretending to know how to read signs, applications, and books. I hid behind my tough exterior, but inside I was wearing the chains of illiteracy.

    I serve a Mighty God. It feels so good to be able to read a book and now even to be able to write a book. No one can tell me how AMAZING My God is, I have tasted of His goodness! I read a quote by Mark Twain that states, "A person who won't read has no advantage over one who can't read." That thought made me read everything I got my hands on. I love words; I desired to expand my vocabulary; so I used my dictionary daily to come up with new words. I bought different bible translations, Strong's Accordance and dictionaries, something I had never even thought I would ever want, but I enjoyed researching. I was learning more about what the word Purpose meant. I wasn't yet sure what mine was at that point, but I knew God would show me.

The congregation Jessica and I were attending was Baptist and I saw a lot of emotionalism in the church. It seemed people only wanted to hear that "God is going to bless you with a new car, a new house, and new shoes. God is going to make a way somehow, God is going to fix it in the sweet by and by". I didn't grasp that concept either, I keep thinking, "Well if God is DONE and it is FINISHED, then He doesn't have to make a way somehow, He's already made the way and it was up to us to hear Him tell us the way". It was just common sense to me, He is the beginning and the end, and He has already been where we are trying to get to in time. He is limitless and powerful, why would it take Him so long to get me a house or car or shoes if that was His plan for me. It seemed to be a place to return every Sunday to get a "quick fix", we dressed to impress then run, shout, fellowship, eat and then go back into the world ill-equipped for the schemes of the enemy.

I thought this should be a place to come and learn more about who we are as people of God. I wanted to know what God said about me as a man and what God wanted me to do for Him. The more God taught me about me, I knew there were other young men who needed the same. What I found out was the church wasn't ready for men like me. They wanted people to look a certain way, talk a certain way and dress a certain way. They didn't welcome people like me that spoke slang, still drunk a beer in public, and who were not abreast of the "Church ABCs". See I hadn't learned how to be bogus or phony and say one thing then do another. In the streets where I grew up, "your word was your bond", and it was all you had.

This was a new world to me, they said out of their mouths, "Come as you are", but when they got there, they didn't accept them exactly the way they were. I shared my testimony in a men's group one night, I thought it was a safe environment for men to be opened and be honest but it wasn't. It was a place where everyone had "arrived" and I found myself ostracized. I learned a very powerful message, "some people don't really believe in the Power of God". They don't believe He can really change, deliver and set free. One of my favorite scriptures is Jeremiah 17:9 "The heart is deceitful, and it is exceedingly wicked above all things, who could know it.

Jeremiah 17:5 "Thus says the Jehovah: Cursed is the man that trust in man, and make flesh his arm, and whose heart departs from Jehovah." I took that to mean; if I put my faith in man or mankind and depart from God, you are cursed. Don't allow people and their opinions to overshadow God's plan for my life.

People's perception is their reality. Whatever a person's perspective is on anything becomes their reality and there is nothing you can do to change it.

But the anointing which you have received of him abides in you, and you need not that any man teach you: but as the same anointing teaches you of all things, and is truth, and is no lie, and even as it has taught you, you shall abide in him(1 John 2:27).

The Spirit is my teacher, it makes sure I hear what I need to hear to proceed on the path it has set for me and it will do the same for you.

"Thus says the Jehovah: Cursed is the man that trust in man, and make flesh his arm, and whose heart departs from Jehovah."

~Jeremiah 17:5~

What I Know Now:

It is the Spirit's responsibility to bring teachers and mentors into your life to move you. It is your responsibility to recognize them and listen. When you refuse the wisdom of an instructor, you have relegated God to only allowing pain to be your teacher.

Chapter Nine
"PURPOSE"

In order for me to even start discovering my purpose and to find me, I had to look inside myself and look closely at all the experiences I had to this point. I had to reexamine my childhood, my teen years, my time in the street and the dope game. I had to be truthful about how those experiences had truly affected me, how they had transformed me into the person I was not, but also how they could be used to transform me into the person I wanted to be, but even more importantly the person God had created me to be. I had decided how I would deal with the opinions of others who thought they knew me. The comments that my mother had made to me out of frustration, the negative self-talk I had spoken to myself. I started to apply the scriptures to my life. I needed to see them come alive in me, so every scripture that I felt was applicable to me, I memorized. I inserted my name in the scripture that spoke to me. Luke 8:9-10 "And his disciples asked him saying, what might this parable be? Richard K. Bennett it is given unto you to know the mysteries of the Kingdom of God, but to others in parables that seeing they might not see and hearing they (meaning other people) might not understand". This scripture says to me, first there are mysteries. Secondly, it is my job to listen to the spirit to figure them out. Thirdly, everyone will not know the mysteries, some people will look but not see, and some people will hear and not understand. Another favorite is Jeremiah 17:5 "Thus says the Lord; cursed be the man that trust in man and make flesh his arm, and whose heart departs from Jehovah." This scripture I kept close to my heart and still do to this day because I was hurt during my journey of Church ABCs. I took people at face value, especially those who said they "loved the Lord". I very quickly find out, everyone who says they know God, He doesn't always know them.

I had dealt with doubt most of my life. Although I gave off the persona of being extremely confident, inside I was a self-doubter. So when I came across Luke 8:12, I hung to it for dear life. I changed the word devil to doubt because doubt was my devil. It says, "Those by the wayside are those who hear, then comes the doubt and take the vision out of their hearts, lest they should believe and accomplish it". That was happening to me, I would hear and become excited, and then someone would say a discouraging word and doubt would set in. Doubt is a purpose killer, a destiny delayer; it is another word for fear. Doubt comes to take the things which you are believing for, right out of your mind. Doubt and distractions become the reason why you never go after what you really want. Distraction can come in many forms; like bad relationships, your friends, even your family or your job. Distractions are anything that hinders you from getting where you want to be. Now add in the fact of not knowing who you are or your true purpose, that's real trouble. I have mentioned knowing who you are several times because it is so important. It is the main thing because when life happens, and you don't know who you are, you become a drifter floating here and there, with no real direction.

If you allow life to lead you to your truth and not establish it for yourself, you will be lead in a direction that is probably not the direction you should be going. There is no one on this earth like you, and that's ok. There is no one who has my fingerprints. I learned that lesson when I was arrested; although I have several brothers, five of them named Richard Bennett; nobody's fingerprints came up except mine. As I get older and wiser, I understand and accept that I am uniquely me. God changed my poverty mindset into a Kingdom mindset. My purpose on this earth is to Just Be who God has created me to be and to encourage others to discover who they truly are and Just Be.

What I Know Now:

I have to seek God for my purpose because He is the only one who knows why He created me.

I cannot push my understanding or my perspective on no one else, but even my family.

I cannot live out my childhood dreams or correct my mistakes through my son.

He has his own dreams and God created him with a special purpose.

My job is to help him discover what that is and nurture it.

"But you are a chosen people, a royal priesthood, a holy nation, God's special possession, that you may declare the praises of him who called you out of the darkness into his wonderful light."

~1Peter 2:9~

Chapter Ten
"CONCLUSION"

After years of driving trucks, I hurt my back and knee, which caused me to be out of work for a few months. While I was off, a friend asked if I would be willing to go to a high school and share my testimony with the students. Of course, I said yes and that was the beginning of me walking into God's purpose for my life. I went to school, I shared my testimony and the students gave me a standing ovation. I was like, "Wow I didn't do anything", but I must admit it felt amazing. I could see and understand them in a way that had never been revealed to me. It was like a light popped on inside of me and I just knew that was what I was created to do. I was asked to visit more middle and high schools and I did. The more I went, the more I realized these children needed more than just my testimony; they need life tools to make their lives better than mine had been. Many of them were from single parent homes and they were just looking for someone to listen. I have learned over the years everyone wants to know they are seen and heard, so I listened. Not only was I there to help them, but they were also there to help me. We need each other, so I continued to visit schools until one day, a doctor I was seeing suggested I started a 5013C. I wasn't sure what that was or how to start it, but went home and told my wife. We researched; prayed about it, filled out the form, sent it to an attorney friend we had met through our janitorial company. He looked it over, called us back and asked who had filled out the application. We told him we had, and he said, "Well, you did a great job, I am going to change one word and send it in, but do not get anxious because they are on hold for six months to a year". We said, "Ok, thank you", and we waited. Three months passed and A Better Tomorrow, Inc. (ABT) was formed. Being the president and CEO of a nonprofit has its own ups and downs. Looking back, I never would have thought a kid from the Westside of town, who could not read would be running a nonprofit organization. Honestly, it was so much easier to just go to the schools, love on the kids without all the drama and politics of grants, foundations, and 990 forms.

    This last eighteen years has not been without its challenges. I learned even when you are genuinely trying to help people and do the right things, there are always hoops to jump through, and trouble lurking around the corner. We have stayed in our lane and continued to do what we said our mission was from day one, "helping youth and young adults discover their purpose through life skills and mentoring". There are always new organizations popping up every day, competing for the same piece of the pie. There are more people at the table ready to eat, but the funding sources basically stay the same. This dilemma causes what is called in the nonprofit world, "mission drift". Mission drift happens when funders decide to change what projects or area of interest they will give money to, so in order to get the money, nonprofits have to shift to that area of interest, or in other words, jump through another hoop, one many have no idea how to do. ABT has always taught life skills education/character building and mentoring; nothing else and thank God, we have developed relationships with not just "funders", but real people who see the vision and make the decision to partner with us to help real people.

I have been through a lot of trials and tribulations, many I must admit to bringing on myself. I have failed miserably at times and have allowed pride and ego to blind me. I have had challenges in my marriage, challenges in my professional life, and life challenges in general, but I believe my biggest challenge came in 2014 when I was falsely accused and arrested. ABT had been chosen to lead the mayor's Violence Reduction Initiative and within a matter of weeks would sign the one-year contract for three hundred and twenty-nine thousand dollars. My picture was on the front page of the local newspaper, as well as on every local television stations. It was an embarrassing and horrible situation. It brought shame to my family and to our organization. ABT lost funding, our grants were frozen, and of course, we lost the contract with the City of Chattanooga. With our finances tied up, it limited the income to the organization. It totally devastated my family financially. We had to let all our staff members go because we were no longer able to pay them, many who had worked for ABT for years and who loved the work and depended on this income. The most devastating part; was the young men who were apart of the program, but who we could no longer help. We had been working with them for three months, while we waited for the council to approve the contract, and in those three months, we had tremendous success. The program had grown from thirteen initially to sixty-four; ranging from ages nineteen to thirty years old. It was frustrating to know that the lie of one police officer could change so many lives. I will share more about this tumultuous time in my next book.

It is now the last quarter of 2018, so for the last four years, my life has been in recovery mode. I have had to piece my life back together. I feel like I am starting all over again. It has been challenging for my family and my marriage. In all these years of helping others discover their truths and who they are, it is at this moment that I find myself in that same place. The only thing I am sure of is GOD! I do not know God in its totality, no one does, but I am sure there is a God. I know for sure I would have never made it this far without God and I know for sure that it is my belief in God that has kept me from basically killing myself.

I do not know what the next year or the next five years will bring, but I do know that God will continue to show himself to me in new ways and I am excited about that. I am listening to God with a fresh ear and a new eagerness. These last four years have shown me who I am, I am not as strong as I thought I was, but my strength lies in God. I have had struggles to remain focused. I know for sure the enemy wants me to give up. I know God has chosen me for such a time as this, for this generation of children who have so many challenges and difficulties. It has been a struggle some days to just get out of bed, but the moment I enter the schools and I see the faces of the young people who I know God has assigned me to, I understand why the enemy is fighting me so hard. If I give up and kill myself or simply stop doing what I do, it leaves my children and the children assigned to me uncovered and unprotected. This is what keeps me going, knowing I am not fighting for myself, but for those without a father, those who do not have someone to instruct and guide them. I cannot lie and say it is easy I have experienced depression and anxiety like never before, but I will not give up, my trust in God is all I have.

I have learned as humans we are all flawed. I recognized that I have in my past been too much of a people pleaser. I looked to people for answers that I needed to look inside myself to find. Some of those flaws led me into addictive behaviors that I wrestled with most of my life, rather it was people, drugs, or whatever; it was just some of life's situations I have been through. I realize one of my faults was not recognizing some of the pitfalls that can happen in every aspect of life, including religion and relationships. Even in marriage and parenthood, there was so much I just did not know. There were a lot of answers I didn't have, but I worked and I am still working it out as I go. Now even after twenty-two years of marriage, I now see marriage in a different light. I believe I could be a better husband and father, although some people say I am doing a great job, I believe there is always room for self-improvement.

Physically, I have put my body through a lot. I have many unnecessary battle wounds, starting with the first gunshot wound at age eight. The enemy did not stop there, there were many more attempts on my life, but God spared me. Many of the mental wounds were self-inflicted, and over the years I have taken on too much of the world I see, trying to figure out my part in making this a better world. The older I have gotten, I have learned I am not called to everyone, it is not my do. God has assigned certain people to me and that is all. I stay in my lane, making sure I do my best to bring God glory.

As I end this book, I would like to reiterate that this is my truth, my reality and my moment of clarity. This book describes much of what I have seen and lived over these fifty-two years of my life. As I bring this book to a close, Donald Trump is the forty-fifth president, when I started writing this book, Barack Obama was the forty-fourth president. I never thought I would live to see a black president. I just did not see that, yet it became a reality, and for me, it was a positive image to see a black family in the white house.

      As I conclude this book, I start on a new venture in life, a new path, a new desire to see my greater self emerge in a way that I have never seen before, and I Thank God for that. I am now fifty-two years old; I still feel I have so much to learn. I know for sure I am growing every day in my understanding of self and God. I have never considered myself a selfish person, I have given of myself, my resources, my time and my family until it was detrimental, but I know for sure it is ok to be a little selfish when it comes to self-care. I have always been good at taking care of others, but never at good at taking care of myself. At fifty-two, it is time I take care of me, physically, mentally, spiritually, and emotionally. If I have not learned anything else from the past four years, you never know how close you are to the edge, until you are just barely hanging on to it. I have to focus on me and focus on hearing God very clearly; being synchronized to His timing and His will for my life. I found out just how controlling I had been when I had no choice but to relinquish all the control to God. It is time I let my scars heal. It is time to release all bitterness and unforgiveness and JUST BE!

I hope that my truth, my story has helped you in some way. If nothing else, stay focused, stay true to yourself and know better is coming.

Have a great day and A Better Tomorrow.

Many Blessings
Richard Kevin Bennett

TO BE CONTINUED

www.ingramcontent.com/pod-product-compliance
Lightning Source LLC
LaVergne TN
LVHW021407080426
835508LV00020B/2476

Bridgette Bastien

What Others Are Saying About This Book...

"Personal experiences leaving us as Overcomers speak volumes. They expose us to God's awesomeness, reminding us that God is real. Bridgette Bastien has penned a plethora of compelling life encounters, causing her readers to join with her in declaring: That had to be God! A refreshing and inspiring book of God working in the lives of everyday people."

- **Fiona Harewood**, Author and Motivational Speaker.

"I truly loved this book. Being a reporter for so many years, I have a hard time reading and listening to stories that do not get straight to the point (like a news article). However, in Overcomer, every word has a purpose. From the very first word, the book jumps right in and gets straight to God's work and the importance of prayer."

- **Gregory Woods**, Journalist and Public Relations Executive.

"Your words have spoken directly to my heart, especially the part about when God says "not yet." I've been in a long waiting game for several years now and God's response has continued to be "not yet." I've felt a little bit like a teacup at times. God has used this book to encourage me."

- **Kerrie Howard**, Pastor's Wife and Dedicated Mother of Three.

Overcomer